THE BOOK OF FIVE RINGS

THE BOOK OF FIVE RINGS

THE CLASSIC TEXT OF SAMURAI SWORD STRATEGY

MIYAMOTO MUSASHI

TRANSLATED BY ASHIKAGA YOSHIHARU ✠ EDITED BY ROSEMARY BRANT

BARNES & NOBLE

NEW YORK

This edition published exclusively by
Barnes & Noble, Inc.
by arrangement with Astrolog
Publishing House Ltd.

2006 Barnes & Noble, Inc.

Cover and text design
by Kevin McGuinness

Calligraphy by Machiko

ISBN-13: 978-0-7607-8457-0
ISBN-10: 0-7607-8457-4

Printed and bound in Singapore

3 5 7 9 10 8 6 4

Photo Credits

Front Cover: Library of Congress

Interior Credits

akg-images: 76–77, 174–75

Art Archive: 28, Photo © Bibliothèque
des Arts Décoratifs Paris/Dagli Orti

Art Resource: 2–3, Photo © Victoria &
Albert Museum, London; 94–95, Photo
© Réunion des Musées Nationaux;
106–07, Photo © Werner Forman;
126–27, Photo © Erich Lessing; 147,
Photo © HIP; 148–49, Photo ©
Victoria & Albert Museum, London

© Astrolog Publishing House Ltd.: 8, 9,
27, 31, 33, 37, 43, 47, 54, 59, 61, 65, 70,
73, 74, 79, 82, 89, 93, 119, 123, 125,
137, 141, 145, 154, 157, 163, 172, 182,
185, 189

Bridgeman Art Library: 86–87, Photo
© Fitzwilliam Museum, University of
Cambridge, UK

Corbis: 153, Photo © Sakamoto Photo
Research Laboratory

© Jim Gilbert: Tsuba rings: 42, 68, 96,
104, 121, 132, 136, 140, 152, 179, 191

Library of Congress: 5, 10, 13, 14, 16, 20,
22–23, 35, 38, 40, 45, 49, 50–51, 53, 60,
62–63, 64, 67, 69, 81, 83, 85, 90, 91, 97,
99, 100, 103, 104–05, 108–09, 110–11,
112, 113, 114–15, 120, 124, 128, 130,
135, 138, 142–43, 144, 146, 150, 158,
160, 161, 162, 164–65, 166, 171, 177,
178, 181, 186, 190, 197

West Point Collection: 4, 6–7, 30, 34,
39, 44–45, 76–77, 80, 84, 88, 92, 98,
101, 102, 133, 134–35, 176–77,
192–93, 200. All Photographs by
Christopher Bain

Contents

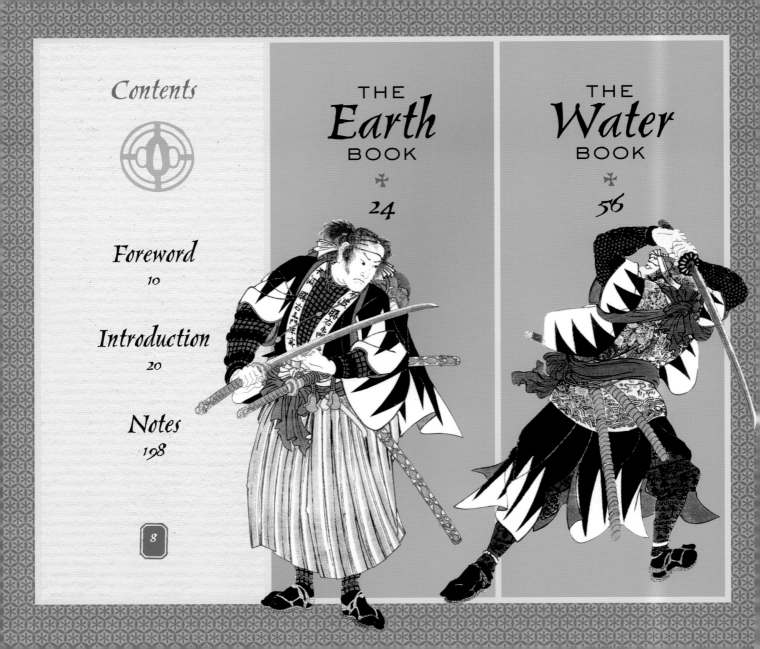

8

THE

Fire

BOOK

✠

116

THE

Wind

BOOK

✠

168

THE

Void

BOOK

✠

194

Foreword

In Japan, Kendo, or the "Way of the Sword," was synonymous with nobility. Ever since the samurai class arose in the tenth century, knowledge of the military arts was considered the highest form of learnedness. Study of Kendo was inspired by the spirit of Shinto and infused with Zen principles. The first schools of Kendo were established in the fourteenth century and continue to exist to this very day. Miyamoto Musashi has long been considered the master of Kendo, and his narrative, *The Book of Five Rings*, its bible.

✤

Miyamoto Musashi is the commonly accepted name of Shinmen Musashi no Kami Fujiwara no Genshin. He was born to a family of former noble lineage in 1584 in Miyamoto, in the province of Mimasaka. Musashi would later adopt the name of this village as his own.

✤

Musashi, who was to become a samurai, was born near the start of what is commonly called the Edo, or Tokugawa era in Japan, which extends from roughly the early seventeenth to the mid-nineteenth century. The original samurai were descendants of aristocratic houses and their rise to power is synonymous with the rise of the Shoguns, clan leaders who served as military generals and

Knowledge of the military arts was considered the highest form of learnedness.

who, by the end of the twelfth century, had usurped control of the country from the emperor.

✣

Musashi lived during a period when the samurai were thought of as the elite of society. In reality however, they had no means of support other than ownership of castles or land, if they even had such. The century before Musashi's birth had been marked by civil war and considerable chaos throughout the country. The gradual attenuation of the lines of noble descent for the samurai, and conflict between warring Shoguns, had led to lawlessness and anarchy throughout the country. In an effort to gain control and bring order, the ruling Tokugawa Shogunate disenfranchised many of the samurai at the same time it relieved the peasantry of their weapons. The samurai were still employed as warriors in times of war, but many were compelled to seek their living as priests, physicians, and teachers. Others became wandering masterless mercenaries known as ronin. Still others, like Musashi, continued along the path of Kendo, searching for the "warrior's ideal."

✣

Legends concerning Musashi begin in his childhood. It is said that his mother died in childbirth, and that he was raised by his stepmother. His father, who may himself have been of samurai stock, was an expert with the jitte, a weapon without a cutting-edge used to deflect swords. Musashi's father was a stern man whose remoteness toward his son likely contributed to Musashi's aggressive spirit. Musashi was an orphan by age nine, and was brought up and educated into his adolescence by his uncle, a priest.

✣

A large and combative youth, Musashi had a seminal experience at age thirteen that set him on the path to becoming a samurai: in hand-to-hand combat, he killed his first opponent, the renowned samurai Arima Kihei, a practitioner of the Shinto Ryu style of combat.

✣

At age sixteen, after another victory in battle, Musashi left home and wandered the country on his own, competing in many battles in order to prove his proficiency as a warrior. That year, he fought in the battle of Sekigahara, the war that helped to pave the way for the ascendance of the Tokugawa Shogunate, the last shogunate of Japan. Musashi fought as a mercenary on the side of Toyotomi Hideyoshi, Tokugawa's opponent. Legend has it that nearly 70,000 warriors died over three days in this battle. Musashi, although seriously wounded, survived.

✠

In 1604, Musashi fought a duel with the master swordsman Yoshioka Seijuro for a supposed slight to his father. Musashi used a bokken, or wooden sword, which was not supposed to kill an opponent. Reportedly, Seijuro was so humiliated by his defeat that after the battle he cut off his samurai's top-knot and never held a sword again. Seijuro's family was not as fortunate. Musashi later killed Seijuro's brother swiftly in a duel he had been goaded into. Seijuro's son is reported to have challenged Musashi to a duel and shown up with thirty men as seconds, armed with guns, arrows, swords, and spears. Musashi had heard in advance of the deception and had hidden in the bushes. Just as the army was preparing to leave, he leapt out, killed Seijuro's son, and slew all thirty men single-handedly. In the chaos of the melee Musashi apparently used two swords, one to kill, and the other to control the enemy's position. This is thought to be the origin of his well-known two-sword technique for fighting.

✠

For most of his adult years, Musashi lived a nomadic life, never marrying, moving across the reaches of Japan in the coldest days of winter wearing scant protection from the elements, and allowing his hair to grow unruly. Legend has it that he never bathed for fear of leaving his weapon unattended. This, combined with his battle scars and disfigurement caused by the skin condition, eczema, is supposed to have given him a wild and formidable appearance useful as strategy when fighting opponents.

✠

From 1605 to 1612, Musashi undertook the Musha-Shugyo, a warrior's quest in which samurai went out into the world and traveled from dojo to dojo (schools for training in the martial arts) to test their fighting technique and hone their skills. During these years he fought many duels using the bokken. On April 14, 1612, he is credited with killing Sasaki Kojiro, master of the nodachi, or two-handed sword. Musashi killed him with a bokken he had made from a boat oar. As the two stood face to face and Kojiro drew his long

sword, Musashi is reported to have called out to him, "You will not need that any longer!" When Kojiro advanced, Musashi went toward him, keeping his own weapon still at his side. As his opponent made the first cut, Musashi came down onto his head from above with the bokken. Many say that after this act Musashi threw down the oar, and brandishing both of his swords over the body of his dead opponent, shouted in victory.

✠

After this battle, Musashi never again used a real sword in battle. He fought only fully-armed opponents with nothing more than a wooden sword. He was unbeatable, and from that time forward, he devoted himself entirely to understanding the Way of the Sword. That same year, he established a fencing school.

✤

Between 1614 and 1615 Musashi fought with the troops of Tokugawa Ieyasu, the most powerful man in Japan, in the siege of Osaka Castle, which was controlled by the clan of Toyotomi Hideyoshi. Musashi was also deeply invested in all aspects of bushido, the samurai code of conduct. In 1615 he served as construction supervisor for Ogasawara Tadanao in Harima province. Musashi perfected his two-sword technique, employing simultaneous use of the katana (long sword) and wakizashi (short sword), as the technique known as Ni To Ichi Ryu. It is speculated that he was inspired in part by observation of the hand movements of temple drummers.

✤

Musashi traveled between 1627 and 1634, at which point he entered the service of Ogasawara Tadazane, whom he fought for in the Shimabara Rebellion, an uprising of Japanese peasants in 1637. As Musashi himself bears witness in his writings, he had achieved enlightened understanding of strategy in 1634, at the age of fifty, following his many battles and six actual wars. During that year, he settled in Ogura. From then until his death he never left the island of Kyushu. After spending six years in Ogura, Musashi was invited to sojourn as a guest in the castle of the lord of Kumamoto. There he taught the military arts, and created ink drawings which are to this day the most famous of their kind in Japan.

✤

In 1643, Musashi retired from society and secluded himself in a cave named Reigando. It was here that he composed the book *Go Rin No Sho (The Book of Five Rings)*. Musashi died in 1645, just a few days after completing the writing of the book.

✤ ✤

R. B.

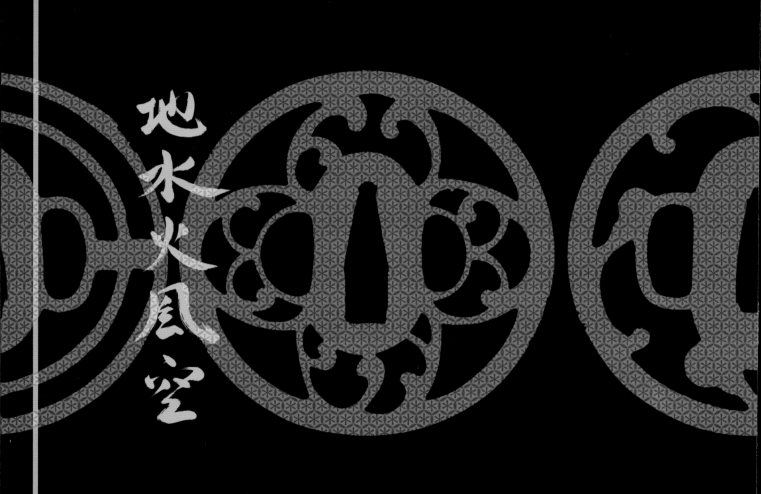

地水火風空

五輪書

THE BOOK OF FIVE RINGS

Introduction

For many years, I have trained in the Way of Strategy which is called Ni To Ichi Ryu. For the first time, I shall now put an explanation of it into writing. I am writing during the first ten days of the tenth month of the twentieth year of Kanei. I have ascended mount Iwato in Kiyusho to extol heaven, to pray to Kwannon, and to go down on bended knee before Buddha. I am a warrior from the province of Harima. I am Shinmen Musashi no Kami Fujiwara no Genshin. I am sixty years of age.

Even in my youth, my heart was captured by the Way of Strategy. My first duel took place when I was thirteen years of age. I beat down a strategist from the Shinto School — Arima Kihei. At age thirteen I struck down the talented strategist Tadashima Akiyama. When I was twenty-one years of age, I went up to the capital and fought many strategists of different origins. I never lost even a single contest.

Afterwards, I went from province to province, dueling with strategists from varying schools. Victory was always mine, even when I faced as many as sixty opponents. This took place when I was between the ages of thirteen and twenty-eight.

When I reached the age of thirty, I looked over my past. My victories previously were not on account of my having mastered strategy. They may have been on account of my natural talent, or perhaps my victories were ordained by heaven, or perhaps the other schools' strategies were weak. Following this, I studied morning until evening, trying to find the principle, until at age fifty I finally came upon the realization of the Way of Strategy.

Since that time I have lived without following any particu-

lar doctrine. With the help of strategy, I have practiced my many skills and talents, without the benefit of any teacher. I did not use the law of Buddha or the teachings of Confucius to write this book. Nor did I use any books or chronicles on military tactics. I take quill in hand in order to explain the true spirit of the Ichi School as it is reflected in the Way of heaven and Kwannon. It is now the evening of the tenth day of the tenth month, the hour of the tiger.

✳✳

五輪書

THE Earth BOOK

Strategy is the Art of the Warrior

Strategy is the art of the warrior. Commanders must utilize this art, and fighters must be familiar with it. There is no fighter in the world today who understands the Way of Strategy completely. There are several Ways. There is the Way of deliverance, according to the law of Buddha; the Way of Confucius, which directs the Way of learning; the physicians' Way of healing; the Way a poet teaches Waka; the Way of the tea ceremony; the Way of archery, and many other skills and crafts. Each person specializes in his area of interest.

✢

They say that the warrior practices in two arenas—that of the pen and that of the sword, and that he must be proficient in both ways. Even if a man does not have an inborn ability to fight, he can become a warrior by consistently practicing each of these Ways.

✢

In general, the Way of the warrior is the brave acceptance of death. Of course, this is true not only for warriors, as even priests, women, farmers, and all sorts of people have sometimes died because of a commitment, or out of shame, but for the warrior it is different.

✢

The warrior is different because by studying the Way of Strategy he learns to defeat

other men. By defeating other individuals in sword battle, or by fighting large numbers together, we are able to achieve power and fame for ourselves or for our lord. This is the measure of strategy.

✠

He can become a warrior by consistently practicing.

五輪書

The Way of Strategy

In China, as well as in Japan, those who implemented the Way were known as "masters of strategy." Warriors must study this Way.

✢

In recent times we have heard of people that carry the title of "strategist." However most of them are simple sword-fighters. The servants of the shrines of Kashima Kantori in the province of Hitashi received teachings from the gods, and established a school based on these teachings. Subsequently, they wandered from land to land, instructing people. This is the new meaning of strategy.

✢

During ancient times strategy was included among the ten talents and seven skills as a beneficial teaching. However it was actually limited only to sword-fighting. The real value of sword-fighting is not seen within the limited confines of technique.

✢

When we look at the world, we see the commercialization of arts. People use objects in order to sell their talents. As with the nut and the flower, the nut has become less important than the flower. In this manner, the Way of Strategy, both among teachers and among students, has become a show of technique, out of their desire to rush the blooming of the flower. They speak about "this Dojo" or "that Dojo." They seek profit. It was once said that "undeveloped strategy is a cause for grief." This saying is true.

✢

There are four Ways through which men can pass in a lifetime: as farmers, as merchants, as gentlemen warriors, and as artisans.

✛

The first is the Way of the farmer. While using agricultural implements, he witnesses the spring turn into the fall, while watching the changes of season.

✛

The second Way is that of the merchant. The wine-maker acquires the ingredients he needs and applies them to his livelihood. The Way of the merchant is to always make a profit. This is the Way of the merchant.

✛

Third is the Way of the gentle-man warrior, who goes his way

armed with the proper weaponry. The Way of the war-rior is to master the wielding of his weapons. If a gentleman does not like strategy, he will not appreciate the contribution of his weapons, and isn't a war-rior at least obligated to be a bit sympathetic to his weaponry?

✛

Fourth is the Way of the artisan. The Way of the carpenter is to develop expertise in the use of his tools. He must first draw his plans with exact measurements, and then carry out the work in accordance with the plans.

✛

The Way of the warrior is to master the wielding of his weapons.

Comparing the Way of the Carpenter to the Way of Strategy

The comparison with carpentry is made by way of the connection with houses—the houses of nobility, the houses of warriors, the Four Houses, the destruction of houses, the thriving of houses, the style of a house, the tradition of a house, and the name of a house. The carpenter uses a master plan for building, and the Way of Strategy is similar in that there is a plan of action. If you wish to learn martial arts, learn and memorize this book. The teacher is like a needle, and memorization is the thread. You must practice unceasingly.

❧

As with the carpenter-overseer, so must the military commander know the natural laws the laws of the land, and the laws of building. This is the way of the overseer.

❧

The carpenter-overseer must know the theory of architecture which governs the towers and temples, and the plans of castles, and he must employ people in order that they will build the houses. The way of the carpenter-overseer is like the way of the commander of the warrior house.

❧

In the building of houses, there must be made a choice of wood. Straight and smooth pieces of timber of attractive appearance are used for the exposed pillars, while straight

The carpenter uses a master plan for building.

宮本武蔵

pieces of timber with slight defects can be used for the unexposed pillars. The very best appearing timber, even if it be a bit weak, can be used for the doorjambs, for doors, for sliding doors, and such. The strongest boards, even if they are coarse and knotted in appearance, can always be used efficiently in building. The weakest boards, or those which are knotted throughout, can be used as scaffolding, and later burned as firewood.

✳

The carpenter-overseer assigns tasks to his workers according to their skills. The floor layers, the sliding door builders, the constructors of doorjambs and ceilings, and so on. The less talented will be put to work at laying the floors, and those with a bit more talent will carve wedges and do other similar jobs. If the overseer knows the abilities of his people well, the final outcome will be good.

✳

The overseer must take into account the skills and limitations of his people. He must mingle among them and never demand of them anything which is not within reason. He must know their spiritual condition and morale, and encourage them when needed. So it is too with the Way of Strategy.

✳

The overseer must take into account the skills and limitations of his people.

The Principle of Strategy

Like a soldier, the carpenter sharpens his tools. He carries his equipment in his toolbox and works under the watch of his supervisor. Using his axe, he fashions pillars and walls; using his plane, he designs flooring and shelves, cuts carvings exactly, and tries to give as perfect a finish as is possible according to his skill. This is the art of the carpenter. When the carpenter develops advanced skills, and is expert at measuring, he himself can become a supervisor.

*

The tasks of the carpenter, when he has tools which cut well, are to build small shrines, writing desks, tables, paper lamps, cutting boards, and lids for pots. These are the specialties of the carpenter. It is similar for the warrior. He must deepen his knowledge of this matter. The carpenter's task is to ensure that his work is stable, that the joints are not loose, and that the work is aligned well so that its parts meet and join, and it is not merely a set of finished sections. This is vital. If you wish to learn this Way, you must go deeply into the writings of this book, one point after another. You must learn this efficiently.

*

The carpenter's task is to ensure that his work is stable.

Chapter

Headings

for the

Five Books

of the

Complete

Book of

Strategy

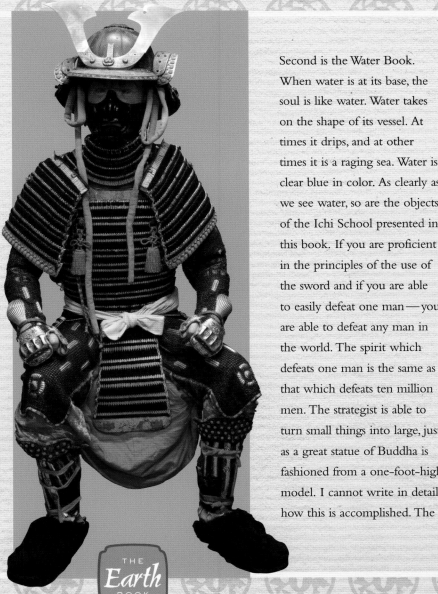

The Way is presented as five books concerning various aspects. These are Earth, Water, Fire, Wind (Tradition), and Void.

✢

The main part of the Way of Strategy from the standpoint of my Ichi School is explained in the Earth Book. It is hard to understand the true Way just from use of the sword. Know the greatest and smallest details, the shallowest as well as the deepest. Like a straight path drawn in the dirt, the first book is called the Earth Book.

✢

The spirit which defeats one man is the same as that which defeats ten million men.

Second is the Water Book. When water is at its base, the soul is like water. Water takes on the shape of its vessel. At times it drips, and at other times it is a raging sea. Water is clear blue in color. As clearly as we see water, so are the objects of the Ichi School presented in this book. If you are proficient in the principles of the use of the sword and if you are able to easily defeat one man—you are able to defeat any man in the world. The spirit which defeats one man is the same as that which defeats ten million men. The strategist is able to turn small things into large, just as a great statue of Buddha is fashioned from a one-foot-high model. I cannot write in detail how this is accomplished. The

THE
Earth
BOOK

principle of strategy is the accomplishment of one thing in order to accomplish ten thousand things. Things from the Ichi School are written in this book, the Water Book.

✦

Third is the Fire Book. This book is about fighting. The essence of fire is its fierceness, whether the fire is small or big; and so it is in battles. The way of battle is identical whether it is against one man or against ten thousand at every side. You must understand the fact that the essence can become small or large. The large is easy to perceive; the small is difficult to perceive. In short, it is difficult

for a large group of men to change its stance, so it's easy to predict their movements in the field. A single man can change his mind easily, which makes it difficult to anticipate his movements. You must know this fact. The basis of this book is that you must train day and night in order for you to be able to make decisions quickly. With strategy, you must concern yourself with making practice part of your daily life so that it never changes. In this way, fighting in battle is put forth in the Fire Book.

✣

The fourth is the Wind Book. This book does not concern

The essence of fire is its fierceness, whether the fire is small or big.

itself with my Ichi School, but with other schools of strategy. When I say "wind" I mean the old traditions, the traditions of today, family traditions, and traditions of strategy. In this way I will be able to explain clearly the strategies which exist in the world. This is tradition. It is hard for you to know yourself if you do not know others. All of the Ways have various side paths. If you learn a Way each day, and your spirit diverges from the path a bit, this bit can with time become a large divergence. You must be aware of this fact. Other strategies are now thought of as simple sword-fighting, and it is possible that you can be sidetracked by this. The advantage of my strategy, although it does include sword-

fighting, rests on a different principle. I have explained in the Wind (Tradition) Book what the other schools mean by "strategy."

✣

The fifth is the Void Book. When I say Void, I mean that it has no beginning and it has no end. Acquiring this principle actually means not acquiring the principle. The Way of Strategy is the way of nature. When you appreciate the power of nature, you know there is a rhythm to each and every situation, and you know also to hit the enemy in a natural manner, to strike him naturally. All of these are things of the Void. In this book, I attempt to show how to follow the true Way according to nature.

✣

THE
Earth
BOOK

The Name
Ni To
Ichi Ryu
(One School,
Two Swords)

Fighters, be they soldiers or commanders, each carry two swords in their belts. In former times, these were called the sword and the long sword. Today, they are known as the sword and the accompanying sword. It is sufficient to say that in our country, for various reasons, the warrior carries two swords in his belt. That is the Way of the warrior.

"Ni To Ichi Ryu" shows the advantage in using two swords.

✣

The spear and the scythe are additional weapons which are used outdoors.

✣

A student of the Way of Strategy of the Ichi School practices from the beginning of his studies, using the sword and the long sword, each in one of his hands. The truth is this: When you are about to battle for your life, you must make full use of your weaponry. It is false not to do this, and to die with a sword undrawn.

If you hold your sword in both hands, it will be difficult for you to wave it freely from left to right. Therefore, my method is to carry the sword in one hand. This does not apply to large weaponry such as a spear or scythe, but to the sword and the accompanying sword, which can each be wielded in one hand. It is cumbersome to hold the sword in two hands when you are on the back of a horse, when you are running on a rough road, in swampy areas, in muddy rice fields, on rocky ground, or among many people. Holding the sword in two hands is not the correct way, since if you are holding

Fighters carry two swords in their belts.

五輪書

a bow or a spear, you will have only one hand free to hold the long sword. But when you have difficulty striking down your opponent with one hand, you then should use both of your hands. There is no difficulty in wielding the sword in one hand; the correct way to learn this is to practice with two long swords, one in each hand. At first it will seem difficult, but everything is difficult at first. It is hard to draw a bow at first, and it is hard to wield a spear at first. As you practice the bow your draw will become stronger. When you practice wielding your long sword, you will achieve the power of the Way and you will handle it well.

✢

As I will explain in the second book, the Water Book, there is no quick way to wield the long sword. The long sword should be handled with a wide movement, and the accompanying sword should be held at the side of the body. This is the first thing you should know.

✢

According to the Ichi School, you can be victorious with either a long weapon or a short weapon. In short, the way of the Ichi School is the spirit of victory, whichever weapon is used, whatever its size might be.

✢

It is preferable to use two swords, instead of only one, when you are fighting a crowd, and especially if you want to capture someone.

✢

These things are not explain-
able in detail. From one thing,
you learn a thousand things.
When you have acquired the
Way of Strategy there will not
be a thing that you can't understand. You must study hard.

✣

The way of the Ichi School is the spirit
of victory, whichever weapon is used,
whatever its size might be.

坂東彦三郎

豊國画図

The Advantage of the Two Aspects of Strategy

The masters of the long sword are called strategists. As concerns the other martial arts, those who master the bow are called archers, those who master the spear are called spearmen, those who master the gun are called marksmen, and those who master the scythe are called scythe carriers. We do not call the masters of the Way of the long sword "longswordsmen," and we do not speak of "accompanying swordsmen." Bows, guns, spears, and scythes are the equipment of the warrior, so they become part of his strategy. To master the long sword means mastering of yourself, and of the whole world, so the long sword becomes the basis of the strategy. The principle is "strategy by way of the long sword." If one masters the long sword, that one man can beat ten men, and so one hundred can overcome a thousand, and a thousand can be victorious over ten thousand. With my strategy, one man is like ten thousand men, so that this strategy is the perfect art of the warrior.

✳

The Way of the warrior does not include other Ways, such as that of Confucius, Buddha, certain traditions, artistic pursuits, and dance. However, although these are not part of the Way, if you know the Way widely, you will find the Way within everything. Each man must pursue his particular Way.

✳

五輪書

*Those who master the spear are called
spearmen.*

THE
Earth
BOOK

The Advantage of Weapons in Strategy

There is a time and place for the use of every weapon.

❖

The most efficient use of the accompanying sword is within a confined and narrow space, or when you are close to your opponent. The long sword is effective to use in all situations.

❖

The scythe is inferior to the spear on the battlefield. With the spear you can take the initiative; the scythe is for defense. Between two men of equal ability, the spear can give a bit of added strength. The spear and scythe each have special uses, but only one of them is especially useful in narrow quarters. You cannot use them for capturing a prisoner. They are vital weapons for the battlefield only.

❖

In any event, when you learn the indoor techniques, you will tend to narrow thinking, and you will forget the true Way. It will be hard to remember actual fights.

❖

The bow is tactically efficient at the outset of a battle, especially when the battle is on an open field where it is possible to shoot arrows quickly from among the spearmen. However, when the enemy is more than thirty-five yards distant, the bow will lose its efficiency. For this reason there are today only a few traditional schools of archery. Today, there is almost no use for this type of skill.

❖

For fighting from within a fort, there is no better weapon than a gun. A gun is also the best weapon for a battlefield in which the sides have not yet engaged one another. The moment swords are crossed however, the gun loses its usefulness.

*

One of the virtues of the bow is that it you can see the arrow and its trajectory and you can adjust in accordance, while the shot of a gun cannot be seen. You must appreciate the importance of this.

*

Just as a horse needs to be fit and strong and have no defect, so must the weapon. Horses must step with power, and swords and accompanying swords must be able to endure repeated use; bows and guns must not have any malfunction. A strong weapon is preferable to one that is merely decorative.

*

You must not have a favored weapon. If you train mostly with one weapon, it is just as bad as if you did not know that weapon well at all. Don't imitate others. Use weapons that you know how to wield properly. It is not a good thing when commanders and soldiers prefer one weapon and avoid others. These things must be deeply understood.

*

Just as a horse needs to be fit and strong and have no defects, so must the weapon.

Timing

in

Strategy

Timing exists in all aspects of the life of the warrior.

There is timing in everything. Timing in strategy does not lead to mastery without a large amount of practice.

�֍

Timing is important in dance and in playing the flute or string instruments. The rhythm is dependent on the timing. Timing and rhythm are also aspects of the martial arts, shooting, archery, gunnery, and horseback riding. In each skill and ability there is timing.

✖

There is also timing in the Void.

✖

Timing exists in all aspects of the life of the warrior, in his successes and in his failures, when he is in harmony and when he drifts from his path. Similarly, there is timing also in the Way of the merchant. In

the rise and fall of his fortunes. Each thing is tied to the rise and fall of the timing. You must learn to notice this. In strategy there are various considerations of timing.

✖

Right at the start, you must know which timing applies and which does not, and you must discern the large things from the small, and the fast tempo from the slow. You must find the appropriate timing. First test the timing of the distance, and the timing of the background. This is the main idea in strategy. It is especially important to know the underlying timing in background; otherwise your strategy will be uncertain.

✖

You will win in battles with the timing of the Void, which rises from the timing of manipulation, when you know the timing of the opponent, and you use a timing which the opponent does not expect.

All of the five books deal mostly with timing. You must train well in order to appreciate this. If you train day and night in the Ichi School strategy which is laid out here, your spirit will rise and broaden. This is the all-inclusive broad-based strategy, and the strategy of dueling which is known in the world.

54

五輪書

This is recorded for the first time in the five books of Earth, Water, Fire, Wind, and Void. Here is the Way for those who want to learn my strategy:

1. *Do not think dishonestly.*
2. *The Way is to train.*
3. *Have knowledge of every art.*
4. *Know the Ways of all professions.*
5. *Know the difference between profit and loss in worldly matters.*
6. *Develop intuition and an understanding of all things.*
7. *See that which cannot be seen.*
8. *Attend even to the seemingly insignificant.*
9. *Do nothing which is useless.*

✠

See that which cannot be seen.

It is important to begin by engraving these principles upon your heart, and training in the Way of Strategy. If you do not look at the broad scale of these things it will be difficult for you to master the strategy. If you learn to understand this strategy you will never be defeated, not even when battling twenty or thirty enemies. The most important thing is to immerse yourself completely in the strategy and to adhere to the Way. And then, you will become able to defeat men in war, to be the victor. By practicing, you will be able to attain full mastery over your body and to influence men with your body. If you train well, you will be able to strike ten men with the power of your spirit. When you have reached this height, does this not mean you are invincible?

✠

In addition, in general strategy, the man who comes out superior will be he who manages his underlings with flexibility, bears himself correctly, governs his country and cares for the people, and preserves the discipline of the rulers. If there exists an invincible way in which to gain honor for oneself, it is the Way of Strategy.

✠✠

五輪書

THE
Water
BOOK

The Water Book

The spirit of the Ichi School of strategy has water as its basis. The Water Book explains methods of victory, according to the long sword part of the Ichi School. There are no words to explain in detail this Way, but it can be understood intuitively. Study this book. Read each word and pore over it. If you do not grasp the meaning deeply, you will be mistaken in the Way.

✻

The principles of strategy are written here in relation to single combat, but you must think in general terms so you will be able to use and understand these principles for battles in which tens of thousands are on each side. Strategy for the Way differs from other strategies for other things. If you make a mistake in the Way, even if the mistake is very small, you are liable to become confused and go in wrong ways.

✻

You will not attain the Way of Strategy by simply reading this book. You must internalize the writings of this book. Do not be satisfied just with reading, memorizing, or copying, but to absorb these things deeply into your heart, you must understand the principles with your body.

✻

Read each word and pore over it.

THE Water BOOK

Spiritual Behavior in Strategy

In strategy, you must not behave spiritually any differently than usual. In fighting, as in day-to-day life, you must be of calm and determined mind. Do not allow your mind to become slack however, or your body to relax. Your body should not relax in correspondence with your mind, and your mind must remain resolute when the body is calm. Keep control of your mind and do not allow your spirit to weaken.

✳

Men of small stature must thoroughly know and understand the body and spirit of men of larger stature. Likewise, large men must understand the spirit of men who are smaller. No matter what your physical

size, always keep your mind in check and know the difference between good and bad actions. Do not allow yourself to be deceived. When you have studied the Ways, you will know the wisdom of strategy.

✳

The wisdom of strategy is unique. Even when involved in difficult battle, never cease to learn the principles of strategy, so that your spirit will remain steady.

✣

In fighting, as in day-to-day life, you must be of calm and determined mind.

五輪書

THE *Water* BOOK

Posture
in Strategy

Assume a posture with head held erect—not with head bowed, not with head hanging, and not with head turned up, down, or sideways. Do not furrow your brow. Do not roll your eyeballs or blink your eyes, but narrow your eyelids slightly. Keep your face composed, and keep the line of your nose straight. Flare your

nostrils slightly. Hold the back of your neck straight. Infuse your neck with strength, and let it travel down by way of your shoulders to the rest of your body. Keep the back erect and do not allow the buttocks to protrude. Infuse your legs with strength from knees to toes. Extend your abdomen so that you do not bend at the hips. Tighten your accompanying sword in your belt against your stomach. This is called "wedging."

In all types of strategy, you must assume this combat posture and make it your regular posture. You must study this well.

Keep your face composed, and keep the line of your nose straight.

Use of the Gaze in Strategy

Use the eyes in a broad manner. There are two aspects of sight—perception and seeing. Perception is strong and seeing is weak. It is vital to see things which are at a distance as if they were close, and things which are close as if they were far away. It is vital in strategy to know the opponent's sword, but not to look at it

and observe its every movement. You must understand
this. Your gaze should be the
same for single combat as for
large battles.

✴

It is important to be able to
see both sides without moving
the eyes. You will not be able
to master this in a short time.
Study what is written in this
book, and practice this gaze
in everyday life without
moving the eyes under
any circumstance.

✴

*It is vital to see things which are at
a distance as if they were close.*

五輪書

THE
Water
BOOK

Holding the Sword

In order to hold a sword, your thumb and forefinger should float, while your middle finger is neither tight nor slack, and the other two fingers are kept tight. It is bad to have slack in the hands.

✤

When you pick up a sword, you must be intent on cutting down your enemy. There should be no change in your grip as you do so. When you come at the enemy's sword to parry it or to strike it down, your thumb and forefinger must move a bit and change their feel. Most importantly, you must keep hold of your sword with the intention of cutting the enemy.

✤

The grip you use for testing of new swords or for fighting is the same. There is no special grip for cutting a man.

✤

Always, with swords as with hands, fixedness is not desirable. The hands must be mobile. A fixed hand is a dead hand. A flexible hand is a live hand. You must keep this in mind.

✤

When you pick up a sword, you must be intent on cutting down your enemy.

Footwork

Floating your toes inward, dig your heels in firmly. The use of the feet should be as usual, whether you move quickly or slowly, or with large or small steps. You should use a normal walking movement. I do not approve of jumping, floating the feet, or inflexible steps.

✠

The "Yin-Yang" foot is very important in the Way. The Yin-Yang foot means never moving only one foot. It means you must move left and right, right and left, when you are cutting, withdrawing, or fending off a slash. You should not prefer to use only one foot.

✠

The use of the feet should be as usual, whether you move quickly or slowly, or with large or small steps.

THE Water BOOK

地水火風空

The Five Stances

The five stances are: Upper, Middle, Lower, Left Side, and Right Side. These are the five. All are for the purpose of cutting down the enemy. There are no other stances save these five.

✠

Whichever stance you assume, you must not think of the stance, but only of the intention of cutting the enemy. Assume a large or small stance according to the situation. The Upper, Middle, and Lower Stances are decisive, and the Side Stances are flexible. The left and right stances should be assumed when there is something overhead or to one side. Decide which to use according to the location of the object.

✠

In order to fully comprehend the stances, you must thoroughly grasp the Middle Stance, which is the preferred stance. The Middle Stance is the main stance. Speaking generally, the Middle Stance is the commander, while the other four stances are the followers of the commander. You must understand this completely.

✠

You must not think of the stance, but only of the intention of cutting the enemy.

The Five Approaches

The five approaches must be learned through repeated training with the sword. When these are mastered, you will be able to offset every attack of the enemy. There is none other than these five approaches, and they must be practiced.

✤

The approaches can be taken with variations in mood and timing. With continuous training you will understand them and you will always win using the Ways of the Sword. Practice faithfully.

✤

The First Approach: Assume the Middle Stance. Encounter your opponent with the point of your sword aimed right at his face. When you make contact with your opponent and he attacks, deflect his sword to the right. Next, hit downwards, so that his sword returns upward, and keep your sword in the downward position. When he attacks again, strike at the enemy's arms from below.

✤

The Second Approach: Assume the Upper Stance and attack the enemy at the exact moment that he strikes out at you. Should you miss, hold the position of your sword as is, and strike again by bringing it upwards as the opponent attacks again. This same strike can then be repeated.

✤

The Third Approach: Assume the Lower Stance. Be ready to attack your opponent from below. When the enemy advances, strike upward at his hands. Your opponent may then try to dash your sword down. If so, let his strike pass by, and then cut his upper arm. Staying in the Lower Stance, you attack at the same moment that he strikes out.

*

Be ready to attack your opponent from below.

The Lower Stance is appropriate for beginners and those more advanced, and should be practiced often with the long sword.

*

The Fourth Approach: Assume the Left Side Stance. Hit your opponent's hands from below, as he attacks. As he moves to deflect your strike, concentrate on hitting his hands, and parry the path of his sword. Cut crosswise from above your shoulder.

地水火風空

This is the Way of the Sword. It is a way to defeat your opponent by parrying the path of his attack. You should carefully study this.

The Fifth Approach: Assume the Right Side Stance with your sword to your right. As your enemy approaches, move your sword from the lower side, to the upper position. Then immediately slash straight downward.

This approach will facilitate your knowing the Way of the Sword well. If you practice this method you will be able to deftly handle a heavy long sword.

Whichever your stance may be, do not focus your attention on the matter of the stance.

I have not written about these five approaches in detail. You must come to know my style and general rhythm and harmony in order to anticipate the opponent's sword's direction. To be practiced in the five approaches, you must train in them daily. By seriously understanding these five approaches, you will be assured of victory by discerning your opponent's intent. This must be considered carefully.

Whichever your stance may be, do not focus your attention on the matter of the stance. Concentrate only on the cut. The stance should be high or low in accordance with the situation. The Upper, Lower, and Middle Stances are decisive.

The Right and Left Side Stances are flowing. The Left and Right Side Stances must be used when there is an obstacle above the head or to one side. The decision to use left or right depends on the location of the obstacle.

The essence of the Way is: in order to understand the principle of the stance, you must grasp well the Middle Stance. The Middle Stance is the heart. If we look at wide reaching strategy, the Middle Stance is the commander, and the four others follow the commander. This should be appreciated.

75

THE
Water
BOOK

The Way of the Long Sword

Knowing the Way of the Long Sword entails knowing how to wield the sword with two fingers, rather than carrying it in the usual manner. If we are well aware of the path of the sword, we are able to handle it with ease.

✤

If you try to wield the long sword quickly, you will be mistaken in the Way. In order to control the long sword efficiently, you must maintain calmness. If you try to wield it speedily, as you would a fan, or a short sword, you will find yourself using by mistake, "short-sword chopping." You will not be able to cut a person with the long sword using this method.

✤

Stance–No-Stance Instructions

Stance-No-Stance means that there is no need for what are referred to as the stances of the long sword. However there are five ways of holding the long sword. The way you hold your sword must be that which makes it easiest for you to cut the enemy well, taking into account your situation and location relative to the enemy. When your energy dips, you can switch from the Upper to the Middle Stance. From there, lift the sword slightly and move back to the Upper Stance. From the Lower Stance you can lift up slightly and move to the Middle Stance as the need calls for it. Depending on the situation, either of the two side stances can become Middle Stance or Lower Stance by moving a bit toward the center.

The most important principle when taking a sword into your hands is to cut down your enemy by whatever means need be applied to this end. Whether you parry, strike, hit, hold, or touch your enemy's cutting sword, you must cut the enemy in the same motion. This is essential. If you think only of hitting, holding, springing at, or striking the enemy, this will not be sufficient to cut him down. You must think first and foremost about performing the motion which will bring about cutting him. You must study this matter thoroughly.

Strategic stance, on a wider
scale, is called "battle array."
These stances are the keys
to victory in battle. Using
inflexible formations is
undesirable. Learn this well.

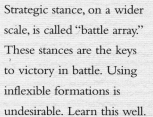

*The most important principle when
taking a sword into your hands
is to cut down your enemy.*

五輪書

To Hit the Enemy in One Count

The significance of One Count is that when you have closed in on the enemy, you hit him as swiftly and directly as you can, without moving your body or changing your mind, so as not to give the enemy time to consider his next moves. Timing the hitting of the enemy before he can decide to withdraw, break, or hit is called One Count.

*

You must practice in order to achieve this timing, so that you will be able to attack instantaneously.

*

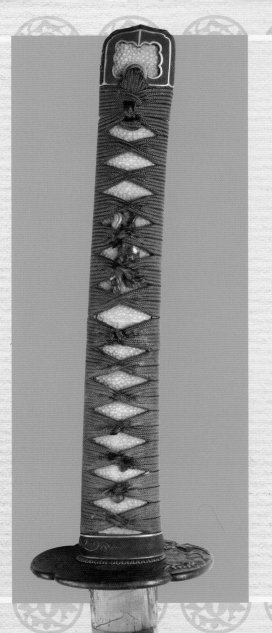

When you have closed in on the enemy, you hit him as swiftly and directly as you can.

Two-Count Timing

When you quickly hit your opponent, and he retreats only to tense for a further attack, you must feint a slash. And then when he relaxes, chase after him and hit him. This is the Two-Count Timing.

✤

It is difficult to achieve this simply by reading this book, but with the help of several lessons you will come to understand it.

✤

When your opponent relaxes, chase after him and hit him.

No Plan– No Concept

With this method, when the enemy strikes and you also decide to strike, you hit with your body and with your spirit, and your hands strike out of a Void, emerging instantaneously. This is the No Plan–No Concept strike.

✳

It is a very effective method of hitting and is often used. You must practice it well in order to understand it.

✳

When the enemy strikes and you also decide to strike, you hit with your body and with your spirit.

Running–
Water Strike

The Running–Water Strike is used when fighting an enemy blade to blade. When he tires and retreats quickly, and tries to hit you with his sword, you must expand your body and your spirit, and cut him as slowly as possible with your long sword, using your power as that of water from a flowing stream. You will certainly be able to cut if you master this. You must discern your enemy's advantage.

五輪書

THE
Water
BOOK

Continuous Cut

When you and the enemy
attack simultaneously, and
your swords meet, hit his
head, hands, and feet, all in
one motion. When you cut
in several places with one
sword stroke, this is called
the Continuous Cut. You
must practice this. It is used
with great frequency. You must
put it into practice until you
are able to understand it.

86

Fire

and

Stone

Cut

The Fire and Stone Cut is used when your sword and the enemy's sword cross and you cut as strongly as possible without raising your sword even the slightest bit. Cut quickly and strongly with your hands, body, and legs. If you practice well you will be able to cut with great force.

Cut quickly and strongly with your hands, body, and legs.

Red–Leaf Cut

The Red-Leaf Cut is knocking the enemy's sword to the ground and taking control of it for yourself. When the enemy stands before you intent on striking, hitting, or parrying, you must strongly strike at the enemy's long sword using the No Plan-No Concept strike or the Fire and Stone Cut. Keep beating down his sword without letting up, until he is forced to drop it to the ground.

If you train this way it will become easy for you to cause the enemy to relinquish his sword. You must practice this over and over.

THE
Water
BOOK

The Body in Place of the Long Sword

This can also be called "the long sword in place of the body." Usually we move the body and sword with synchronization in order to cut the enemy. However, in accordance with the system of cutting which the enemy is using, you can attack him first with your body, and cut him afterwards with your sword. If it is not possible to move his body, you can first cut with the long sword, but generally you should hit first with your body and then cut with the sword. You must investigate this well and practice this type of hit.

You can attack him first with your body, and cut him afterwards with your sword.

The Cut and the Slash

The Cut and the Slash are distinct from each other. The cut is decisive, and done with a brave spirit. The slash is simply a touching of the enemy. Even if the slash is a strong one and the enemy dies, it is still a slash. With your cut, the spirit is resolute and set. You must understand this. If at first you slash the hand or foot of your opponent, you must afterward strongly cut him. Slashing is similar to touching. When you come to realize this, it becomes recognizable. Study this thoroughly.

The Body of the Chinese Monkey

The Body of the Chinese Monkey is the tactic of not stretching out one's arms. The spirit is to rush in quickly as the enemy prepares to strike, without extending your arms even a bit. You purposefully do not stretch out your arms; the idea is to approach and strike with your entire body. When you come within arms' reach of the enemy it will be easy to approach with your body. Investigate this well.

The Glue
and Lacquer
Body

The essence of the Glue and
Lacquer Body tactic is to come
close to your enemy's body, and
to effectively stick to him. When
you approach the enemy, attach
yourself firmly to his head, his
body, and his legs. There is a
tendency to stick only to the
head or feet and to leave out the
rest of the body. You should stick
firmly leaving no space between
your body and the enemy's.
Think this over carefully.

Contest

of

Height

The Contest of Height means that when you are in proximity of the enemy you must strive to maintain the height advantage, with no let-up. Extend your legs, stretch your hips, and stretch your neck, keeping your face aligned with his, intent on winning, and on being taller. When you feel you have the height advantage, hold strongly to it. You must make great effort to learn this.

When you feel you have the height advantage, hold strongly to it.

Applying Glue

When you and your enemy strike simultaneously, you must attach your sword to his and hold your swords together so that they do not separate, and you absorb his blow. The spirit of sticking to your opponent's sword as if glued is not to hit out with great strength. Rather the point is to make it impossible for the swords to separate easily. Do this as calmly as you can, while adhering strongly to the enemy's sword. The difference between "gluing" and "entanglement" is that gluing is steadfast and entanglement is weak. This must be appreciated.

When you and your enemy strike simultaneously, you must attach your sword to his and hold your swords together.

The Body Strike

水

The Body Strike is delivered when the enemy lets down his guard momentarily. Turn your face slightly sideways, and strike at the enemy's chest, while thrusting your left shoulder outwards. Come toward the opponent with the intention of repelling him, and strike as mightily as possible, in rhythm with your breathing. If you succeed with this method of closing in on the enemy, you will be able to throw him back a distance of ten or twenty feet. You can strike a fatal blow in this manner. Practice faithfully.

Three Ways to Parry the Enemy's Attack

There are three ways to parry an attack:

Push the enemy's sword to your right, as if toward his eyes, as he attacks.

or

Thrust the enemy's sword toward his right eye, as if snapping his neck.

or

When you have a short sword, move in quickly towards the enemy and hit his face with your left hand.

❋

These are the three methods of parrying. Always keep in mind that you can use your left fist to punch at the enemy's face. It is necessary to practice hard for this.

THE
Water
BOOK

Stabbing

the

Face

Stabbing the Face means that when you are in confrontation with the enemy you set your spirit with the intention of stabbing your sword into his face, with the tip of your long sword

following the line of the blade. If you remain intent on stabbing your long sword into his face, his face and body will be pulled into control. Once the enemy is under control, you will have several opportunities to beat him. You must concentrate on this. When during the battle, the enemy's body becomes controllable, you can quickly be victorious, and so you mustn't forget to stab the sword into his face. You should acquire this important skill through practice.

You mustn't forget to stab the sword into his face.

宮本武蔵

Stabbing
the Heart

When during a fight there are obstacles above or to the sides, making it difficult to cut, you must thrust at your opponent. You must stab your long sword into the breast of the enemy without letting the point of

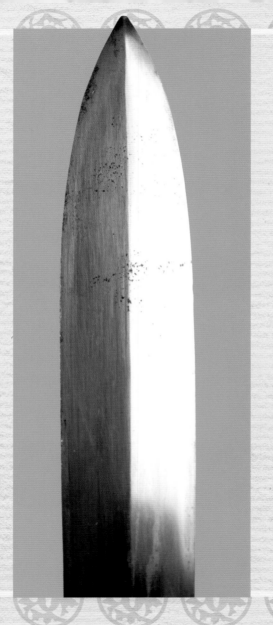

your sword waver, with the blade of the sword before the enemy's eyes and with the intent to deflect his long sword sideways. This principle is very efficient should you become tired or for some other reason your long sword has difficulty cutting. You should understand the use of this method.

When during a fight there are obstacles above and to the sides, making it difficult to cut, you must thrust at your opponent.

Scolding "Tut-Tut"

When the enemy tries to counterattack just as you attack, you again counterattack from below, and try to hold him down. You cut with a quick rhythm, scolding the enemy. As you thrust up, yell *"tut!"* and cut. Yell *"tut!"* again.

The timing for this cut is used repeatedly in exchanges of blows. You should yell the Scolding "Tut-Tut" at the same moment that you raise your sword as if to thrust at the enemy. You must learn this well by training repeatedly.

When the enemy tries to counterattack just as you attack, you again counterattack from below.

The Slapping Parry

The Slapping Parry is carried out when you are up against the enemy and you absorb his attacking cut with your long sword with a "tee-dum, tee-dum" rhythm, while slapping at his sword, and cutting him.

⁜

The spirit of the Slapping Parry is not simply slapping fiercely or parrying, but slapping the enemy's sword in accordance to his attack, when your intent is first and foremost to cut him quickly. If you understand the timing of the slapping, even during the most difficult of sword battles, the blade of your sword will not be repelled, even slightly. You must study this to understand it.

⁜

THE Water BOOK

There Are Many Enemies

The There Are Many Enemies
method is put into practice
when you are one fighting
against many. Draw your sword
and also its accompanying
sword, and use the Right and
Left Side Stances. The idea is to
go after the enemies from side

to side, even though they may come from all four directions.

✣

Pay attention to the order of their attacks, and counter those who attack first. Take in your surroundings well, and make note of the attacking order, and cut right and left alternatively, with two swords. Waiting is not desirable. Always return quickly to the two Side Stances, cut the enemy as he advances, and repel him to the direction from which he starts to attack. Whatever you do, you must crash the enemy together, as if you were tying a line of fish. When it seems they are piled together, cut them fiercely, giving them no room to move.

✣

THE
Water
BOOK

The Advantage When Exchanging Blows

熊坂長竹蛇

You can learn to win by using the strategy of the long sword, but to explain it clearly in writing is not possible. You must train industriously in order to know how to be victorious.

✻

According to the oral tradition, "The true Way of Strategy is revealed by the long sword."

✻

You can learn to win by using the strategy of the long sword.

THE
Water
BOOK

One Cut

水

You will be able to win using the One Cut. It will be hard to achieve this without learning strategy thoroughly. If you practice well in this way, strategy will flow from your mind and you will have the ability to win according to your will of mind. You should practice thoroughly.

✤

Direct Communication

The spirit of direct communication has been transmitted as the true way of the two swords. According to oral tradition, you must train thoroughly and make it part of your body.

✻

The Ni To Ichi School teaches the Ichi School way of sword-fighting. In order to learn to win using the long sword strategically, first you must learn the five stances and the five approaches, and to incorporate the way of the long sword into your body. You must be in harmony with intent and rhythm, and wield your sword with natural movements of your body and legs, as they work together harmoniously with your mind. Being able to beat one enemy or two

will depend on your knowledge of the martial arts.

✠

Study what is in this book, one
line at a time, and practice with
opponents, until you grasp fully
the principle of the Way.

✠

Patiently and deliberately, learn
the value of all of this, taking
part in combat occasionally.
Know your enemy's mind,
whoever he may be.

✠

You make a journey of a
thousand miles by taking
step after step.

✠

With study and over time,
you will achieve the spirit of a

*Patiently and deliberately, learn the
value of all of this.*

THE
Water
BOOK

warrior. You will surpass today what you accomplished yesterday, and tomorrow you will go further still, until you will be able to vanquish more highly skilled men. Train according to this book, and don't allow your mind to get off track.

*

No matter what opponent you may manage to defeat, it will not be the true Way if you do not do it according to these teachings.

*

If you retain these principles in mind, you will know how to beat even tens of opponents.

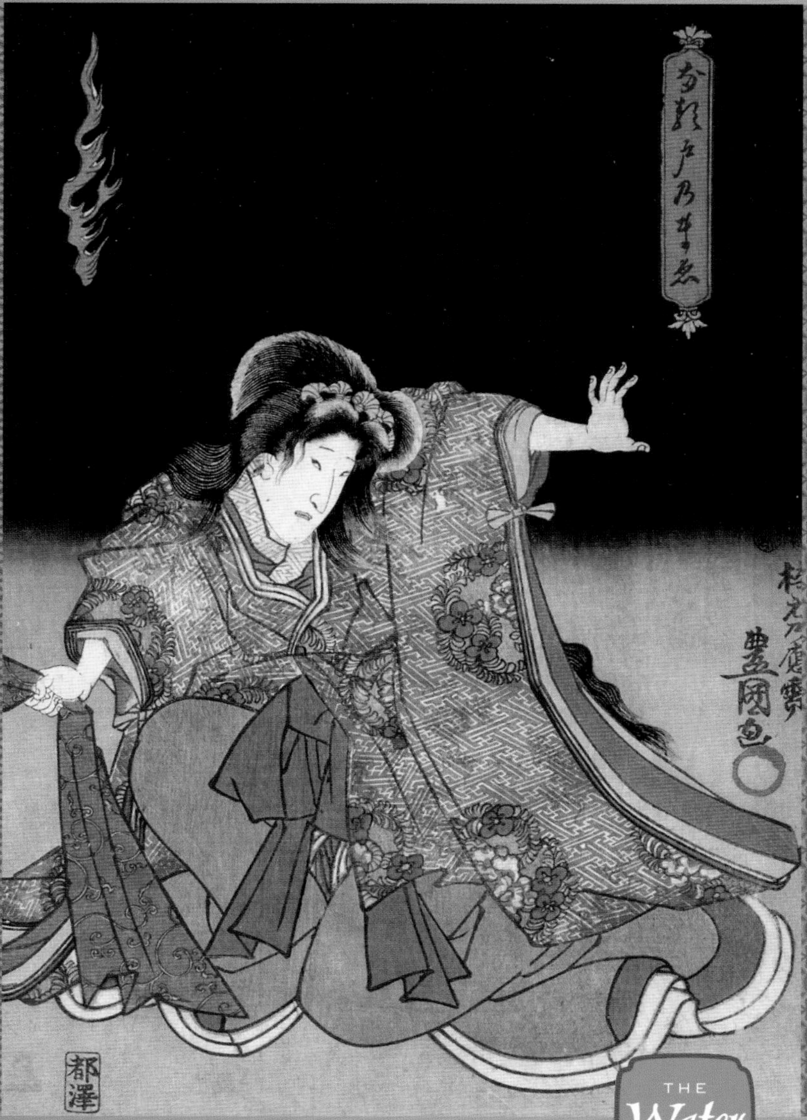

You need also a strong knowledge of swordsmanship, so mind that you allow yourself many practice battles and duels.

With study and over time, you will achieve the spirit of a warrior.

五輪書

THE
Fire
BOOK

The Fire Book

In the Fire Book of the Ichi School of strategy, I refer to fighting as fire.

❋

Firstly, people tend to think of the less important aspects of military strategy, such as the three- to four-inch advantage of the wrist over the fingertips. They think a contest is decided within the span of the fore-arms, like the folding of a fan. They become expert at the insignificant matter of dexter-ity, and concentrate on minor aspects such as practicing hand and leg movements with a bamboo sword.

❋

With my strategy, training for killing opponents is done over the course of many battles. The meaning of life and death is discovered through practice in the way of the sword, and knowing the strength of our opponent's attack and under-standing the ways of the edge and the back of the sword.

❋

You do not need to employ insignificant techniques when you are dressed in full armor. My Way of Strategy is a proven method of victory when you are battling for your life against one man, or against five, or ten. There is no difference between the principles with which one man beats ten, or with which a thousand beat ten thousand. You must consider this. Of course, it is not ordinarily pos-sible to train with a thousand or ten thousand men. However, you can learn your enemy's strategy, and his strengths and weaknesses, by training by yourself with sword in hand, and you will absorb the principles of beating ten thousand men in this manner.

✤

Whoever desires to become expert at my strategy must study hard and train constantly, morning and evening. He must polish his skill, be independent of self, and attain a superb ability. He will then attain miraculous power.

✤

This is the result of practicing my strategy.

✤

The meaning of life and death is discovered through practice in the way of the sword.

五輪書

THE
Fire
BOOK

About Place

火

Ascertain the conditions of your environment. Stand with the sun behind you, and if you cannot have the sun at your back, then stand with the sun to your right side. Indoors, stand with the light from the entrance behind you or to your right side. Stand so that there is no obstruction to your rear, and so that there is room to your left. Your right side is taken up with your sword stance. At night, keep fire behind you and the light from the entrance to your right, so as to be able to see your enemy. Look down at your opponent by standing in a slightly higher place. The Kamiza of a house is an example of such a high place.

✢

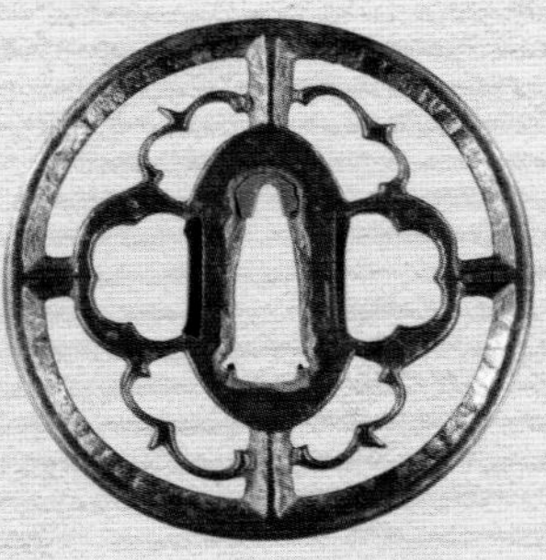

Always chase your opponent into places of awkward footing.

As you take up the battle, you must chase your enemy to your left, moving him towards uncomfortable places. Try to keep his back facing those difficult places, so that he cannot see and evaluate the situation. Keep chasing him until you trap him. Indoors, chase him toward a door, porch, pillar, or so on, all the while keeping him from seeing his predicament.

✢

Always chase your opponent into places of awkward footing, where there are obstacles to his sides, and so on. Assess the characteristics of the place in order to find advantageous positions. It is important to study and practice this thoroughly.

✢

Three Ways to Engage the Enemy

The first method is to attack. This is called Ken No Sen, or to set him up.

✠

The second method is to hold him off as he attacks. This is called Tai No Sen, or waiting for him to take the initiative.

✠

The third method is to attack at the same time as the enemy. This is called Tai Tai No Sen, or to both accompany and forestall him at once.

✠

These are the only methods to begin the fight. There are no others. It is possible to be victorious quite quickly if you take the lead at the beginning, so this is very important in strategy. Each of these initiatives has differing characteristics. You must take up the best one for the situation. You must sense the enemy's spirit so that you will know which strategy will beat him. I cannot write about this in great detail.

✠

The first method is to attack.

宮本武蔵

Ken No Sen

When you take the initiative and attack at the outset, stay calm and move in quickly and suddenly. You can move in

strongly, while keeping some of your energy in reserve to forestall your enemy.

✣

It is also possible to advance with a strong resolve of mind, while moving your feet more quickly than usual. This fast and strong approach will overwhelm your opponent.

✣

Alternatively, you can attack with a calm mind and spirit, strongly maintaining the feeling and the intention of victory and cutting down your opponent.

✣

All of these ways of initiative are Ken No Sen.

✣

When you take the initiative and attack at the outset, stay calm and move in quickly and suddenly.

宮本武蔵

Tai No Sen

As your opponent approaches, remain totally serene, and pretend to be weak. As the enemy approaches, make a sudden movement as if you intend to escape by jumping sideways, and when he relaxes at this, you can rush in and attack strongly. This is one possibility.

Another way is as the enemy attacks, you attack even more ferociously, claiming victory out of the chaos.

These ways of initiative are Tai No Sen.

Tai Tai
No Sen

Allowing the enemy to attack
quickly, you attack with resolve,
but calmly. As he nears you,
move to strongly defeat him.

✳

If the enemy is serene, be
watchful of his movement.
Using a floating movement of
your body, attack with him as he

approaches and attacks. Attack quickly and make a strong cut.

✠

This way of initiative is Tai Tai No Sen.

✠

The three ways of engagement are difficult to discuss in words. You must research diligently the things I have written here. You do not always need to be the first to attack, and you must assess each battle accordingly. If the enemy is first to attack you can control him. You will win if you are effective at forestalling your opponent, so practice diligently in order to learn this.

✠

As the enemy nears you, move to strongly defeat him.

Pushing Down the Pillow

Pushing Down the Pillow is the technique of not allowing your opponent's head to come up. In the Way of Strategy, it is bad to be led around by the enemy. You must lead the enemy around. Your enemy will also be bearing this in mind, but he will not be able to detain you if you forestall him first. You must stop him as he comes in for the cut. Check his advance by pushing down

his jabs and free yourself from engagement with him. This is what is meant by Pushing Down the Pillow. When you fully understand this Way you will perceive the enemy's efforts and you will advance in time to suppress them.

✠

The main thing in strategy is to disallow your opponent's efficient actions, while allowing his useless actions. But if you do only this you will be on the defensive. First, act according to the Way, and thwart the enemy's plans and then you command him. When you are able to do this, you will have mastered strategy. You must practice hard at Pushing Down the Pillow.

✠

Crossing

Over

Crossing Over means crossing a body of water at a strait, or traversing thirty-one miles of sea at a crossing point. There are many events in a lifetime where a man is required to "cross over." You must sail across even though it means leaving your friends behind. You must have knowledge of the route and of the abilities of your vessel. You must be familiar with the route you will travel, and study weather conditions. You set sail when winds are favorable. You may have to drop your sails before reaching your destination and row the rest of the distance.

✣

If you achieve this spirit, you will use it in all of your dealings in life. You must always have the intention to cross over.

✣

In the military arts, Crossing Over is vital. In battle, perceive the strengths of the enemy, and keeping your own abilities in mind, cross over when you see you have arrived at the proper crossing point. By doing this, you behave as a good captain setting sail on the sea. When you see that the crossing is successful, you can feel at ease. By Crossing Over, you will be victorious, as you have attacked the enemy at his weakest point, and attained a definitive advantage.

✣

Always maintain the intent to cross over, whether fighting a small or large battle. You must research this thoroughly.

✣

There are many events in a lifetime where a man is required to "cross over."

Knowing the Times

Knowing the Times means understanding the tendency of your opponent's strength or weakness in a particular battle. Is he feeble or forceful?

✢

Discern the condition of your opponent's men, and deploy your men in accordance. This will give you an advantageous position, and you will win using this strategy.

✢

When engaged in a duel, you must measure the enemy's ability and take stock of his weaknesses and strengths. You must take into account his School of Strategy. Note his timing and his rhythm, and attack when he least suspects it, using his time variations to your advantage.

✢

Knowing the Times, once your ability to use it is fully honed, will allow you to see into your opponent's mind and understand his intentions. This will allow you the opportunity to win. You must thoroughly study this.

✢

Knowing the Times will allow you to see into your opponent's mind and understand his intentions.

Stamping
on
the
Sword

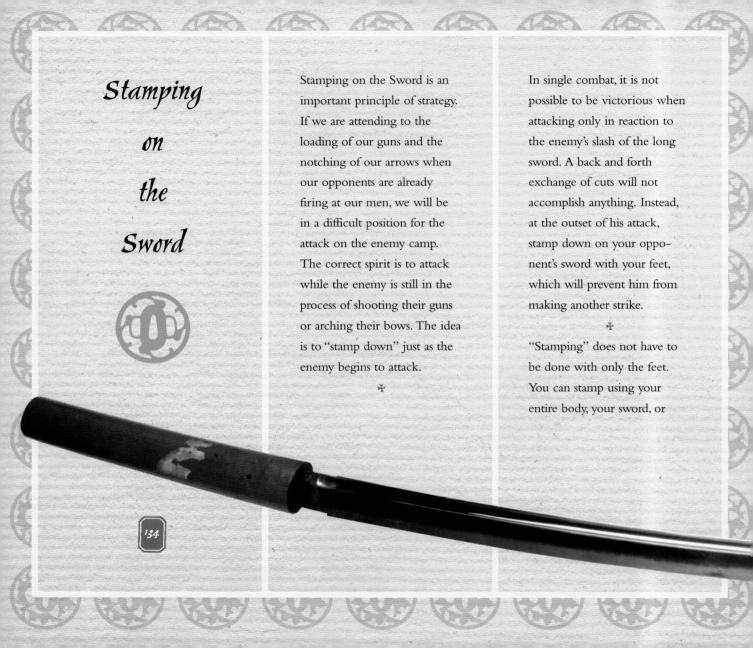

Stamping on the Sword is an important principle of strategy. If we are attending to the loading of our guns and the notching of our arrows when our opponents are already firing at our men, we will be in a difficult position for the attack on the enemy camp. The correct spirit is to attack while the enemy is still in the process of shooting their guns or arching their bows. The idea is to "stamp down" just as the enemy begins to attack.

✢

In single combat, it is not possible to be victorious when attacking only in reaction to the enemy's slash of the long sword. A back and forth exchange of cuts will not accomplish anything. Instead, at the outset of his attack, stamp down on your opponent's sword with your feet, which will prevent him from making another strike.

✢

"Stamping" does not have to be done with only the feet. You can stamp using your entire body, your sword, or even your mind. Stamp in the spirit of not allowing the enemy to rise for a second attack. Stamping on the Sword should be done at the very moment of your opponent's attack. This is the very essence of holding off the enemy in every sense. You must gain a deep understanding of this.

Stamping on the Sword should be done at the very moment of your opponent's attack.

Knowing Collapse

火

Anything can collapse. A house, a body, or your enemy will collapse when its rhythm is upset.

✠

In a military conflict involving large numbers, when you perceive your enemy beginning to collapse, you must continue to pursue him in order to take advantage of his demise. Do not allow him to escape or to have a chance to recover.

✠

In one-on-one combat, you can sometimes discern that your enemy is losing his rhythm and is about to collapse. Do not allow this opportunity to pass, as he may use your negligence as a chance to recover. Concentrate on your enemy's collapse, and keep at him, attacking relentlessly so that he will not be able to recover. You must attack with a sure and strong spirit. You must cut the enemy down with force and might. You must accomplish this. You must cut the enemy completely so that he cannot recover. You must understand how to beat down the enemy thoroughly.

✠

When you perceive your enemy beginning to collapse, you must continue to pursue him.

Becoming the Enemy

Becoming the Enemy means thinking of yourself as if you are in the opponent's body.

Becoming the Enemy means thinking of yourself as if you are in the opponent's body. People tend to think that a robber who has taken refuge in a house is a powerful enemy. But if you look at the situation from his point of view, you will see that he feels the whole world is against him, and that he can never escape. The man trapped in the house is like a pheasant. The man who will move in to arrest him is like a hawk. This must be appreciated.

✠

In large-scale military action, it is a mistake to think of the enemy as strong, as this will tend to make you cautious. If you have a good army, if you have a good understanding of the principles of strategy, and if you deeply believe that you are about to be victorious, you should have nothing to worry about.

✠

You must also use Becoming the Enemy in single combat. Do not think of your opponent as a master of strategy, or you will surely be defeated. You must understand this deeply.

✠

Releasing Four Hands

Releasing Four Hands is used when you and the enemy are in the same frame of mind, and the contest is coming to a draw. Let go of this feeling decisively, and you will be victorious by using another method.

✢

In military actions with many participants, when the four-hands spirit reigns, you must continue in this vein or you will lose, and your army will take losses. You must discard this spirit, and overtake the enemy by changing to a surprise tactic.

✢

In single combat, if you feel you have arrived at a four-hands situation (stalemate), you must change your frame of mind, and switch to a proper technique as befits your situation. You must be able to discern the proper action.

✢

Overtake the enemy by changing to a surprise tactic.

Moving
the Shade

Moving the Shade should be
used when you cannot detect
what is in the enemy's mind.

※

In large-scale military actions,
when you cannot see your
opponent's position, you must
behave as if you are about to
make a ferocious attack. This

will allow you to assess his intentions. You will then be able to defeat him easily, using the proper method depending on what you see are his resources.

✴

In one-on-one combat, if your opponent is in the side or rear approach and you cannot read his intention, pretend to come at him, and he will then show you his long sword. He will believe he has read your intention. Pay attention to what he shows you, and you will win. If you neglect to do this, your timing will be off and you will lose. Think hard about this.

✴

In large-scale military actions, when you cannot see your opponent's position, you must behave as if you are about to make a ferocious attack.

Holding Down the Shade

When you are able to read your opponent's mind and strategy, you can use Holding Down the Shade. During large-scale actions, after the enemy makes his first strike, you must vigorously put down his attack. He will then retreat. When he does, you can change your tactic, and beat him by fending him off with a Void presence of mind.

✤

In single combat, you must suppress the enemy's intention to win by using timing, and defeat him by suppressing and using this timing. You must study hard at this.

✤

When you are able to read your opponent's mind and strategy, you can use Holding Down the Shade.

Infecting

There are many things which are infectious. When we are sleepy, we pass on our yawning to others. Time can also be passed on.

✤

When fighting a large-scale battle, if the enemy seems rushed or agitated, you must not be infected by this. Behave with complete calm, and act unaffected. The enemy will see this and become relaxed also. When you see you have successfully infected the enemy with relaxation, you can defeat him by moving in decisively with a Void frame of mind.

✤

When in single combat, you must relax your body and mind, and when the opponent is infected by this and relaxes himself, you can attack vigorously and quickly, and you will fend him off.

✤

"Getting him drunk" is a similar idea. You infect the enemy with a weak, slack, or careless frame of mind. You must understand this thoroughly.

✣

"Getting him drunk" is a similar idea.

THE
Fire
BOOK

Throwing Your Enemy Off-Balance

Many things cause us to lose our balance. Some of these are fear of danger, being in a difficult position, and fear that something is about to creep up from behind. Research this well.

In large-scale strategy, you must try to cause your enemy to lose his balance. You will do this by attacking by surprise, when the enemy does not expect it. While his mind is still undecided as to how to proceed, you can make use of your advantage and defeat him.

In one-on-one combat, you must begin slowly, and then attack strongly without warning. Do not allow your opponent to recover from the surprise. While he remains agitated, you must move in for victory. Learn the way this feels.

To

Frighten

Fear is common in life, and it is caused by the unexpected.

In large-scale military battles you will not frighten your opponents by what they can see freely with their eyes. Rather you will frighten them by making sudden noises, or by the illusion that a small force is large. You may frighten them by coming at them by surprise from the side. These are all frightening actions. You will be victorious if you use the change in the enemy's rhythm when he is frightened.

In single combat, it is also possible to defeat the enemy by taking him by surprise and frightening him using your body, your sword, or your voice.

You must research this well.

It is also possible to defeat the enemy by taking him by surprise and frightening him using your body, your sword, or your voice.

美盾八競

To Be Absorbed

When you are in the grip of
a battle with your enemy and
you do not see a way to make
progress, you must try To Be
Absorbed into your enemy and
become one with him. When

you are intermingled and entwined with your opponent, choose a suitable technique to employ to bring about victory. In battles involving many as well as in one-on-one combat, you can often win by using knowledge of being absorbed, if you are careful to remain engaged and not to disentangle which would cause you to be defeated.

✣

You must understand this well.

✣

When you are intermingled and entwined with your opponent, choose a suitable technique to employ to bring about victory.

Injuring the Corners

When trying to move something heavy, you will have difficulty if you push directly against it. You must "injure the corners" in order to make progress.

✣

In large-scale battles, you must hit the corners of the opponent's force. If you can injure the corners you will be able to defeat the entire army. When the corners have been struck, follow this by a full force attack on the enemy.

✣

When fighting one on one, you can easily win if you bring about your opponent's collapse. You do this by wounding the "corners" of his body, which will weaken him and cause him to slacken. You must research this idea intently, as it is of importance for winning.

✣

THE Fire BOOK

Causing Confusion

To "cause confusion" means you make the enemy lose his resolute state of mind. In broad military situations you should try to confuse the enemy on the battlefield. If you make him uncertain, he will think of varying possible actions and ask himself, "Should I go there? Here? This way? That way? Faster? Slower?" If the opponent is of a confused spirit, you can certainly be the victor.

In single combat, you must confuse the enemy by using various techniques, as the opportunities arise. Feign thrusting or cutting, and pretend that you are about to rush in toward him. When your opponent shows signs of confusion, you can easily attain victory.

✠

This is a vital principle of battle. Research it well.

✠

To "cause confusion" means you make the enemy lose his resolute state of mind.

地水火風空

The Three Shouts

There are three shouts: before, during, and after. Shouting is important, and you must shout as the situation warrants. Your voice is a vital element. The shout has energy.

�֍

In large-scale battles, we must shout as loudly as we can, at the start of the confrontation. While the battle is being waged, we use a lower pitch, letting out a shout as we attack. When the fight is over, we let out a loud shout declaring our victory. These are the three shouts.

✖

In one-on-one combat, we pretend to begin to cut, and shout *"Ei!"* just as the fight begins. This will encourage your enemy to start to move. After the shout, cut your enemy with your long sword.

✖

After we have beat down the opponent, we shout again to herald our victory. This is the "sen go no koe," which means the before and after voice. Never shout while flourishing the long sword. Shout during the fight in order to enter the rhythm.

✖

Research this carefully.

✖

Shouting is important, and you must shout as the situation warrants.

THE
Fire
BOOK

Mingling

In large battles, when the armies are facing one another, attack your enemy's strongest areas, and as they begin to retreat, regroup and attack still another of his strong points, along the sides of his force. This is done in a zig-zag manner.

*

When one man is fighting against many, this principle is very important. Attack the enemy's force in one area, or force them to retreat, and then, after having gotten into a rhythm, attack one after the other of his strong points, zig-zagging left and right, as if on a winding mountain path. Taking stock of your enemy's frame of mind, never think of retreat, and continue to attack strongly.

*

In one-on-one combat, use this same technique and take note of the enemy's strong points.

*

Mingling means advancing toward the enemy and becoming taken up within his forces, while never retreating at all.

*

You must understand this well.

*

Mingling means advancing toward the enemy and becoming taken up within his forces.

Crushing

You must crush the enemy, regardless of your feeling that your own strength is great, and regardless of your perception that he is weak. This is a vital frame of mind.

✳

In large battles, when the enemy is weak because he has few men, or when he has many men but they have fallen into confusion, you will win by

Crushing. You must crush them strongly, giving no opportunity for recovery. Do not allow them to rally and take a breath. You must be intent on victory and never let them regain position.

✣

In single combat, when the opponent has less ability than you, or if he has fallen out of rhythm and is beginning to retreat, you must immediately and totally crush him, with no regard for his circumstances. It is vital that you do not allow him to recover.

✣

You should deeply research this.

✣

You must crush them strongly, giving no opportunity for recovery.

Mountain and Sea

Mountain and Sea means that you should not repeat the same thing over and over when fighting your enemy. Sometimes you will have to use the same technique twice, but you should endeavor not to do it a third time. Once you

have failed at an approach, you will likely fail yet again if you attempt to do the same thing. When you try to do again something you have already tried unsuccessfully, and then you fail at it a second time, you must next try a different method.

✣

Surprise your enemy with a different tactic. While your opponent thinks about mountains, you should attack like the sea; while he thinks of the sea, you must attack like a mountain!

✣

You must understand this deeply.

✣

Hitting Bottom

When engaged in battle with the enemy, at times it seems we will win by using the principles of the Way of Strategy, when in reality we are winning only on the surface. If the enemy's spirit is still strong, you may defeat him only shallowly, while he remains undefeated deep beneath the surface. When this happens, we must use the strategy of Hitting Bottom in

order to undo his spirit and demoralize him to the very depths of his being.

✳

Hitting Bottom can be accomplished by using the long sword, by using the body, or by using the mind. It is difficult to generalize this principle.

✳

When we have succeeded in penetrating the bottom of the enemy's spirit, we can relax our intention. If we have not yet hit the bottom, we must remain in a strong state of mind.

✳

You must practice Hitting Bottom in large-scale battles as well as in single combat.

✳

Renewing

You must renew your mind and begin as if over again.

Renewing is called into play when the battle is a stalemate and you and your opponent are making no progress. Then you must renew your mind and begin as if over again. Let go of your former rhythm and begin with a fresh and different one. Renewing means that when we are in a deadlock with the opponent and cannot change anything about our circumstances, we instead change our mindset and win by using a new tactic.

✤

It is vital to understand Renewing in large-scale strategy as well.

✤

Research this well.

✤

THE
Fire
BOOK

Rat Head, Ox Neck

火

Rat Head, Ox Neck strategy is used when we are fighting an enemy and both of us have become so preoccupied with the smaller details that the battle is not progressing. The Way of Strategy includes our having both a rat's head and an ox's neck. When we have become stuck in the smaller points, we must know how to change agilely to a larger spirit. We must know how to move between large and small.

✠

This is one of the vital points of strategy. The warrior must be able to think in this spirit concerning all aspects of his life. You must always use this strategy—in large-scale combat as well as in single combat.

✠

The Commander Knows the Soldiers

The principle of The Commander Knows the Soldiers is applicable in every type of fight, and is necessary to fulfill your desire to win.

❊

You must consider the enemy as if he is one of your own soldiers. As such, you will command him to move around according to your intentions. When you are of a mind that you order the enemy as you would your soldier, you will become the commander of your enemy. You should master this principle.

❊

You must consider the enemy as if he is one of your own soldiers.

THE
Fire
BOOK

Letting Go
of the Hilt

There are several aspects of Letting Go of the Hilt. There is the spirit of winning while not holding a sword. There is the spirit of holding the long sword and not winning. These aspects cannot be written down. You must practice them well.

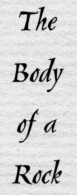

The Body of a Rock

When you have completely understood the Way of Strategy, you will have the ability to become as if your body is a rock. You will be stuck, and untouchable. This is The Body of a Rock.

✳

You are unmovable. This is according to the oral tradition.

✳

What I have recorded above are my thoughts concerning the Ichi School of sword fighting. I have written them down here for the first time, as they came to my mind. They have been written in a rather confused order, as they are difficult to express clearly. They should be used as a guide for any man who wishes to learn the Way of Strategy. I have given my whole heart to the Way of Strategy ever since my youth, and I have trained diligently with my hands, my body, and my spirit, in the attitudes of battle. When we observe other schools of strategy, we see that their theories concentrate on the technical aspects, and although they may develop skill, they do not have the true heart of the fighting spirit at all. Men who study these other ways may believe they are indeed training both the body and spirit, but their bad influence is never ending. Therefore the true Way of Strategy is dying out and becoming extinct.

✳

The true Way of sword battle is the art of fighting your enemy and defeating him, and nothing more or less than this. If you will understand and be true to the wisdom of my Way, there will never be any doubt that you will be victorious.

✳ ✳

When you have completely understood the Way of Strategy, you will have the ability to become as if your body is a rock.

THE *Fire* BOOK

五輪書

THE
Wind
BOOK

The Wind Book

Part of strategy is being familiar with the Ways of other schools. I record the principles of the other styles of strategy in this book, which I call the Wind Book.

*

We would not be able to fully understand my Way of Strategy of the Ichi School without knowing the other traditions. Observing the other schools, we notice that some of them specialize in the strength of using a very long sword, while others specialize in the shorter version of the long sword, the Kodachi. Some of the schools instruct in the use of many various techniques for wielding the long sword—some using the surface approaches, and others using the "inner" approaches.

*

I have demonstrated clearly in the body of this book that none of these is the true Way. I have shown all of what is good and right and all of what is bad and wrong, based on the true principles.

*

My Ichi School idea is fundamentally different. The other schools consider this a performance, or a means of making a living. They grow their flowers, or paint decorations for sale. This is not the Way of Strategy.

*

The other strategists concern themselves only with the ways of handling the long sword and the stances of the body. These, however are not all that is entailed in winning. They are not the essence of the Way.

*

I write down the drawbacks of the other schools, one by one, in this book. You must study this thoroughly in order to appreciate the advantages of my Ichi School.

*

Other Schools Which Use Long Swords

五輪書

Some of the other schools have a preference for using the extra-long long sword. From my point of view, these schools should be seen as weak. They do not uphold the principle of defeating the enemy in any way possible. They believe the extra-long long sword, because of its length, will afford them a win while maintaining a distance from their opponent.

✳

There is a saying: "A hand just one inch longer has the advantage." But this saying has no bearing in martial arts, and is quoted by those with no experience with strategy. Since they

It is not good to be preoccupied with the length of the sword.

are of weaker spirit and knowledge of fighting, they are dependent on the distance of the longer sword, which allows them to fight without knowing the principles of strategy. This should be seen as a weakness.

✳

There may be some justification for using the extra-long long sword at times, but certainly we can be victorious if we use the short sword and have no long sword. It is not good to be preoccupied with the length of the sword. This might make you doubt your own strategic ability. One should not have a preference for a certain length of sword.

✳

It has been said since long ago that the large and small dwell together. There is nothing wrong with the long sword, but the preference for it is mistaken.

✳

I compare the long sword to a fight with many enemies, and the short to smaller combat. Many times the few can win out over the many!

✳

If you are inclined to prefer the longer sword, and you are forced to fight in a small space or indoors and you have access only to the shorter sword, you will not be able to use your best strategy. If the opponent comes in close to you, it will be difficult to wield the longer sword. The sword will become cumbersome, and will put you at a disadvantage, compared to a fighter who holds a short sword. Also, take into account the fact that some men are simply stronger than others.

✠

In my Way, I do not approve of the narrow minded or pre-conceived. You must study this principle.

✠

I compare the long sword to a fight with many enemies.

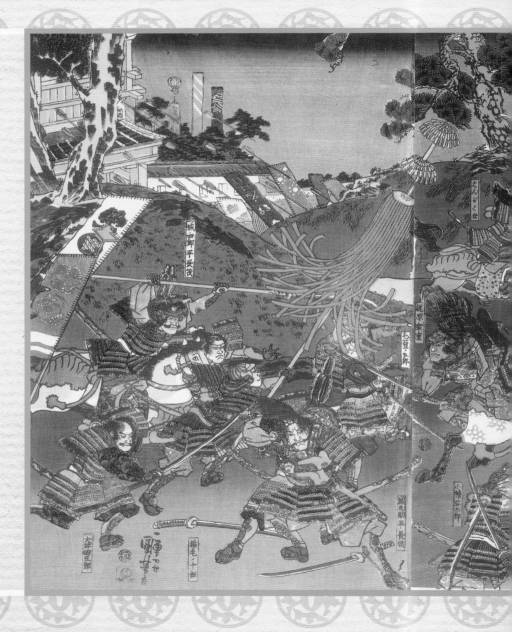

Use of the Long Sword in Other Schools

We should not differentiate between strong and weak swords. When you wield your sword roughly, in a strong frame of mind, your sword work will be rough, and your cutting coarse, which will make it difficult to win.

✠

If you are preoccupied with the strength of your sword, you will attempt to make overly strong cuts, and you may fail to cut at all. Even when testing a sword, it is not right to cut too strongly. When you are fighting an opponent, you should not bear in mind the strength with which you will cut him. Think solely of cutting him down and beating him. Be intent only on killing him. You should not try to make strong cuts, nor should you intend to cut weakly. Be concerned only with killing your enemy.

✠

If you depend on your strength, you will invariably use too much force against the enemy's sword. This will cause your own sword to follow through the movement too hard, and to be carried along. Do not believe the saying: "The Strongest hand wins."

✠

In large battles, when your soldiers are strong and are depending on their strength to carry them to victory, and the enemy also has strong troops who are thinking similarly, the battle will be equal and difficult.

✤

You must use the correct principle of my strategy to win. Do not pay attention to unimportant details. Remain intent on using your wisdom and knowledge of my strategy to win. Study this idea.

✤

When you are fighting an opponent, you should not bear in mind the strength with which you will cut him.

THE
Wind BOOK

Use

of the

Shorter

Sword in

Other

Schools

178

Always using the shorter sword is not the true way to win.

✤

The words Tachi and Katana have been used historically to refer to long and short swords. Men of great strength can easily wield the longer sword lightly, so being able to wield lightly is not the reason for choosing a shorter sword. For length, they carry spears and scythes. Some men believe they will be able to cut the enemy with a shorter sword by rushing him by surprise while he brandishes a longer sword. This is not true thinking.

✤

Aiming to attack the enemy at an unguarded moment means we are completely on the defensive. This is not desirable

as we may become entwined with the enemy. You will not succeed in jumping into the midst of a hoard of opponents and winning. Some fighters believe that the shorter sword gives them the ability to leap agilely around the enemy, cutting him, but actually they will have to defensively parry the enemies' swords, and will be totally on the defensive. This is not the true Way.

✤

The right way to win is to chase your opponent with a strong and erect body. This will put him on the defensive and confuse him, so that he will jump away. The same is true in large-scale battles. The main idea of strategy is to attack the enemy in large numbers so that he quickly falls. The other schools teach evading and retreating as if it was the usual thing to do. They become used to these actions, and allow their enemies to command them. The Way of Strategy is direct and true. You must pursue your enemy intently and force him to obey your mind.

✤

You must pursue your enemy intently and force him to obey your mind.

THE *Wind* BOOK

The Use of Many Techniques by Other Schools

I believe the other schools teach many methods as a sales technique, in order to be able to sell their ways to beginning fighters. The purpose of selling is considered anathema to the spirit of true strategy. Studying numerous ways of cutting down a man is confusing. First of all, killing is not natural to mankind. There are not so many methods—whether for a woman, a child, a fighter, or for whomever—to cut down a man. There are the methods of stabbing and slashing, but there are no other methods. There is no need to speak of fine details.

⁂

However, depending on where you are located while fighting, you may face obstructions from above or to the sides, and you will need to carry your sword without drawing it. There are five methods (directions) for this. Other than these five, there are no other methods to cut which are part of the true Way of Strategy. Twisting, bending, and jumping are completely useless for cutting the enemy. In my strategy, the body and mind are straight, and the enemy should be made to twist and bend. The right thinking is to attack the opponent when his mind is warped, and yours is straight.

⁂

You must investigate this well.

⁂

Depending on where you are located while fighting, you may face obstructions from above or to the sides.

The Use of Other Approaches in Other Schools

It is a mistake to place too much importance on the use of the different approaches of the long sword. It has been seen in the past as in the present, that there is no particular correct way to fight. It is essential to move your enemy into difficult situations.

⁑

Approaches are used in situations when you will not be moved. If you are guarding a castle in battle array, you must stand strongly, giving the impression that you are immovable even with fierce aggression. However, in battle, you must take the lead and attack

Intending to attack on the offensive is different from being attacked and on the defense.

the enemy. Thinking about approaches will put you in a position waiting to be attacked. You must understand this.

⁑

In the Way of Strategy, you must always take the initiative. You must use the offensive rather than be of a mind to be attacked. Attack strongly, and parry the opponent's attack skillfully. You must put him at a disadvantage, and throw him into confusion.

⁑

When you understand this Way you will see that using approaches is taking the defensive, and you will know that this is wrong. In my Way, I have the spirit of approach-no-approach, which means no approach needs to be taken.

At the start of a large-scale battle we observe our enemy's troops, taking note of their numbers and other details of their circumstances.

⁑

Intending to attack on the offensive is different from being attacked and on the defense. Bearing up under an attack strongly, and fending off the enemy well, can be likened to constructing a wall of spears and scythes. You will have to pull out pieces of your wall in order to attack the enemy. You must examine this principle.

⁑

The Use of the Eyes in Other Schools

The use of the eyes is variable according to the different schools. Some fix their eyes on the enemy's sword, and others fix their eyes on the enemy's hand. Still others fix their eyes on the enemy's face, on the feet, and so on. If you choose one place to fix your eyes, you can become confused, and your art of strategy will be compromised.

✠

I will explain the reason for this. Players of ball games never fix their eyes upon the ball. They play well by virtue of their moves on the field. When you have become accustomed to something, you do not need to fix your eye upon a certain object. Musicians and acrobats who must balance several objects do not fix their eyes in one place — they succeed by having practiced until their art is familiar and habitual.

✠

In the Way of Strategy, you will become accustomed to fighting many opponents in many battles, and you will have mastered the appraisal of the enemy and the ability to read his mind, and the position of his sword. In the true Way, fixing the eye means looking into a man's mind and understanding him.

✠

In battles involving large numbers of troops, you must perceive the abilities of your opponent's

men. Use "perception" rather than eyesight to "see." Perception means concentrating on the enemy's spirit, taking in the conditions of the battlefield, and observing the course of the fight as it changes.

In single combat, do not fix your eyes on any single detail. As I said previously, if you concentrate on details you will neglect the important factors, and you will become confused. This will make it impossible to win. Research this principle well.

If you choose one place to fix your eyes, you can become confused.

五
輪
書

Use

of the

Feet in

Other

Schools

There are several ways to use the feet. These include: floating feet, jumping feet, springing feet, stamping feet, and crow's feet. From my point of view, none of these are satisfactory for my Way of Strategy.

❖

I do not like floating feet because the tendency is for the feet to float anyway — the Way is to make the feet step firmly instead.

I do not like jumping feet, since it will encourage a jumping habit, which fosters a jumpy spirit. There is no real reason ever to jump repeatedly, so it is bad.

❖

Springing feet, too, will foster a mind intent on springing, which makes the fighter indecisive.

❖

Stamping feet is a form of "waiting," which I particularly disapprove of.

❖

Other than these methods, there exist several forms of stepping quickly, such as crow's feet.

❖

You may at times have to battle an enemy on marshy ground, in a swamp, in a river valley, on stony terrain, or on a narrow road. In these situations you will not be able to jump about and take quick steps.

❖

In my Way, there is no change in the way you use your feet. I walk just as I normally do in the street. You must move according to your perception of the opponent's rhythm, always controlling your feet, and adjusting your speed accordingly.

❖

In large battle situations your footwork is very important. This is because if you attack quickly without learning the enemy's mind, you will use a wrong rhythm, and you won't be able to win. If you attack too slowly, you will fail at bringing the enemy to collapse, and the contest will not be decided quickly. You must not allow the enemy any hope of recovery, by taking advantage of his moments of confusion. You must practice this often.

❖

The Use of Speed in Other Schools

Speed is not an aspect of the Way of Strategy. We use the word speed to denote whether things are fast or slow, according to whether they remain in rhythm. A man who masters strategy does not appear fast.

✤

If a person walks fast on a road, covering fifty miles in a day, this does not mean he is capable of running unceasingly from morning till night. Even an unskilled runner may run all day, but without going very far.

✤

In dancing, the most talented can sing at the same time that they are dancing, but an unskilled dancer will lose his rhythm when he confuses their spirit in this manner. The tune "old pine tree" when played on a leather drum, is very mellow, but when an unskilled drummer attempts the rhythm, he may beat ahead or behind the tempo. A very skillful drummer can play quickly, but if the drum is beat too hurriedly the timing will get lost. Drumming too slowly is also not desirable. The most skillful will not lose their timing. They are always exacting, and never appear hurried. By studying this example, the principle can be learned.

✤

Going fast is not done in the Way of Strategy. The reason is that when fighting in marshes or swamps or wetlands, it will be difficult to move the feet and body quickly. Also, you will not be able to cut quickly with your long sword in this situation. If you do try to cut quickly, you will fail to cut at all. This should be appreciated.

✳

In battles with large numbers of fighters, it is wrong to have a fast or slow intention of mind. The spirit should be that of holding down the pillow, so that you will not slow down at all. Or, if your opponent is too fast, you must respond on the contrary, with calm. Train well at this intention.

✣

A very skillful drummer can play quickly, but if the drum is beat too hurriedly the timing will get lost.

Interior

and

Exterior

in Other

Schools

Interior and exterior are not aspects of strategy. In the other arts, the concepts of interior and exterior refer to entrance into the inner mind or secret traditions. However, in combat, there is no such thing as dueling on the surface or cutting an opponent's interior. In teaching my Way of Strategy, I teach tactics which the student can grasp easily. I try to explain the deepest concepts in a way that can be comprehended by the student as he progresses. The student will have to learn by experience. I never refer to "the entrance to the interior."

✻

I perceive the knowledge of my student, and I teach him the Way simply and directly.

In this world, if you are in the mountains, and you wish to go further into the depths of the mountain range, you will come out through the entrance again!

✻

In this and other analogies, there are aspects of the interior, and benefits of the entrance. However, in matters of military arts, it is not revealed what is concealed and what is open.

✻

Accordingly, I do not pass on my Way by use of contracts or rules. I perceive the knowledge of my student, and I teach him the Way simply and directly, while trying to have him reject the disadvantages of the other schools. I gradually instruct him on the true Way of Strategy.

✻

My way of teaching my strategy is straightforward and honest. You must train diligently.

✻

I have tried to write down an outline of the other schools' strategies, in the above nine sections. I could now write specifically about each one of these schools, from the entrance to the interior, but I have not named the schools or laid out their main principles. This is

THE
Wind
BOOK

because each branch of each school has its own explanation and understanding of the principles. Men differ in their opinions, and there are various interpretations of each matter.

No one person's conception is the truth about any school.

I have discussed the main tendencies of the other schools concerning nine points. If we look at them objectively, we see that people tend to prefer either a long sword or a short sword, and that they concern themselves with details and strength in large and small matters. You can therefore understand why I do not discuss the entrances of the other schools.

In my Ichi School there is neither entrance nor interior. There is no inner meaning in the sword approaches. You must simply remain of true spirit to understand the virtue of strategy.

You must simply remain of true spirit to understand the virtue of strategy.

五輪書

THE
Void
BOOK

The Void Book

In this Void Book, I will record the Ichi Way of Strategy.

❖

The Void is where there is nothing or any form. Man cannot have knowledge of this because it is nothing. Since we have knowledge of what is, we therefore know what is not. That is the Void.

❖

People sometimes think that which they do not understand is the Void. This is not true. This is confusion.

❖

Military strategists and those who study war sometimes think that whatever they do not understand is the Void. But this is not the true Void.

❖

In order to master the Way of Strategy, you must study the other martial arts, and you must not abandon the Way of the warrior at all. You must set your mind upon practicing every single day, hour by hour. You must develop the double spirit of the heart and the mind. And you must appreciate the two-fold use of perception and eyesight. When your mind is clear, and there are no clouds of confusion, this is the True Void.

❖

Before you understand the True Void, you may think you have gained understanding either through Buddhism or through everyday thought. When you realize the true Way, you will understand that each of us sees the various ways through different eyes. Seeing these other ways is to reject the true Way.

Make sure you base your practice on a wide foundation, and
learn a large number of martial
arts. This way, you will understand the Void as the Way, and
you will see the Way as the Void.

✳

The Void is good, and contains
no evil.

✳✳

Shinmen Musashi

*The Void is good, and contains
no evil.*

Notes

(Numbers in notes refer to page,
paragraph, and line.)

Introduction

21.1.2. *Way:* The Japanese Character for
Way is read as "Michi" or "Do." It refers
to the entire life of the warrior, his faith-
fulness to the sword, and his position in
the Tokugawa bureaucracy. The Way is the
road of life, to which God points the way.

21.1.2. *Strategy:* "heiho," a word originating
from Chinese meaning "military strategy."

21.1.11. *extol heaven:* "ten," or "heaven,"
here refers to the Shinto religion.

21.1.12. *Kwannon:* The Buddhist god of
mercy.

23.1.11. *spirit:* "shin" or "kokoro" which
means heart or soul (or spirit), a feeling or
manner of behavior.

23.1.16. *hour of the tiger:* The years, months,
and hours were named using the ancient
Chinese Zodiac system.

The Earth Book

26.1.14 *Waka:* A poem of thirty-one
syllables. The word means "song in
harmony."

26.1.15 *tea ceremony:* The drinking of tea is
studied in schools and is a ritualized subject.

26.1.16 *archery:* The bow was the main
weapon of the samurai during the earlier
era. Only later was the bow replaced by
the sword. Archery, like the tea ceremony,
was a ritualized pursuit.

26.2.2–3 *that of the pen and that of the sword:*
During the Tokugawa period, young people
were educated in the writing of the Chinese
classics and in correct use of the sword.

26.3.2–3 *brave acceptance of death:* The
fighter is obliged to choose death when
the choice is life or death. A man who
continues to live after a failure at his
intended tasks is but a coward. The
defeated man must die. This is the most
important instruction in the Way of the
warrior. The man who is aware that death
may arrive this day, and who thinks of
himself as a lifeless vessel, is one with the
Way of the warrior, and is able to live a
life without failure and to carry out his
tasks as required. The principle of bravely
accepting death is the main point in the
philosophy of the *Hidden Pages*, which
was written in the seventeenth century
by a samurai from the province of
Nanshima-Han.

29.2.5–6 *shrines of Kashima Kantori:* The
Shinto shrines that contain the preserved
traditions of the original Kendo schools.

29.4.14 *Dojo:* The room in which a certain
subject is studied. "The hall of the Way."

29.5.1 *four Ways:* The social order in Japan
was extremely strict. There were four
major social classes—the highest being the
samurai, which included landlords, senior
government clerks, warriors, foot-soldiers,
and those with official jobs. The second
class in the hierarchy included farmers,